IMAGES OF ENGLAND

Fareham

The Lower Quay, winter 1895-96.

IMAGES OF ENGLAND

Fareham

Alice James

NONSUCH

SWANS AT FAREHAM CREEK.

For my grandchildren

First published 1996
This new pocket edition 2005
Images unchanged from first edition

Nonsuch Publishing Limited
The Mill, Brimscombe Port,
Stroud, Gloucestershire, GL5 2QG
www.nonsuch-publishing.com

British Library Cataloguing in Publication Data.
A catalogue record for this book is available from the British Library.

ISBN 1-84588-146-X

Typesetting and origination by Nonsuch Publishing Limited
Printed in Great Britain by Oaklands Book Services Limited

Contents

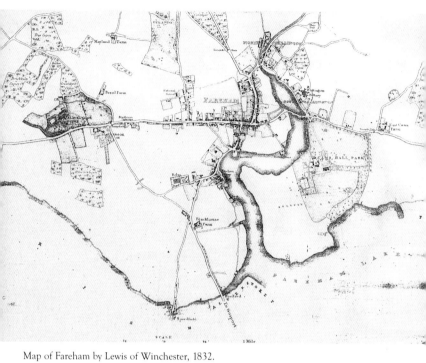

Map of Fareham by Lewis of Winchester, 1832.

Introduction

This book of old photographs is an attempt to fill in some of the gaps left by my previous books and is partly a response to requests from members of the younger generation to whom the war is, if a memory at all, a distant one.

I am well aware of the fact that changes were occurring even before the war, with the growth of housing estates, but I can think of few market towns which have had their character changed so much as has Fareham.

Now a borough, several outlying villages and settlements form part of the modern town and so, due to the character and limitations of the book, it has been necessary to confine the pictures mainly to the effects of changes to 'old' Fareham. I must therefore, in advance, beg forgiveness for so many missing areas due to limitations of the size of the book. I am well aware of the absence of Wallington, Fontley, the Turnpike area and North Hill with its brickmaking and St Christopher's, Knowle and many others. Sometime perhaps it might be possible to write a book called 'Outside Fareham'. Material is certainly there in abundance.

History is being made all the time and I shall include quite recently taken as well as older photographs so that newcomers can get some idea of the essential Fareham, a port and a market town, quiet except on Mondays, market day, when one could walk along West Street and be sure to meet one friend or acquaintance and so I hope that this book will succeed in its purpose and might even bring about a demand for 'more please'.

To set the scene, old Fareham in southern Hampshire lies at the head of Portsmouth harbour where the River Wallington enters the sea in a large tidal estuary. It has grown tremendously since the Second World War but it is, however, my intention to keep to 'old Fareham'.

When I first think of Fareham, probably unlike many people, I think of the harbour and the many quays and wharfs along the shore estuary. Visible from my house on the Gosport Road it was possible to see almost the whole life of maritime Fareham. Much silting up during the war has resulted in the larger ships from Scandinavia and the rest of Europe being replaced by gravel boats and dredgers, yachts, motor boats and even water skiers, but the constantly changing scene is fascinating.

It was common, and still is possible in spite of alterations, to see at one glance a ship from the Continent being unloaded while at the other quay another ship is being loaded. No longer alas, are handmade tiles from Fontley being loaded to go to Belgium – it took a whole week to load those tiles. Nor is one likely to see smuggled matches coming from Belgium! The flour mill at the Lower Quay is still there although now redundant but there is still the building of smaller boats at See's just around the corner. At high water, boys still dive into the creek and the yacht races are there to be enjoyed.

Looking across the water were once the farmlands of Cams Hall, recently converted into a golf course, but nearby there is cricket and football on the recreation ground, a large area of land donated in perpetuity to the people of Fareham by Squire Deane of Fairfield House. Cutting across all this is the railway with its splendid viaduct.

As George Privett once said 'what tales these shores could tell!': smuggling (not necessarily over yet), poaching on Cams Estate (a brace of pheasants with their necks wrung), the large ships for the Royal Navy being built, like the *Jesus* on the shores of the creek, and the King being informed, during Stuart times, that Fareham was 'as good and safe a harbour as Chatham'. Out in Fareham Lake Napoleonic prison hulks gave way to hospital ships, later to captured submarines, to the 'mothball' fleet and now to a peacetime sailing channel. The hospital, pre-Haslar, was situated at the Lower Wharf, the buildings are still there but taken over by the Yacht Club, the Sea Scouts, various industries and housing. Also there is the huge naval burial ground, now largely forgotten and unknown except when a skeleton is dug up! An ex-resident once remarked that 'there may be no skeletons in the cupboards, but most of the houses have their own private skeleton in the gardens!'

So Fareham, once scathingly termed 'that fischer village' by Leyland, shows its rich history to those willing to look. A big market centre is now mainly a commuting area with much residential development. Most of the old shops have disappeared. Many of the changes have not been popular with longtime Fareham residents and I fear – judging from my correspondence – that many of the new buildings are even less popular. Ever-changing Fareham indeed!

Alice James
Wickham, 1996

A scene from Gosport Road, showing the greater part of the main harbour, the Town Quay, the Lower Quay and the flour mill.

One

Fareham – The Port

'See's' advertisement, from one of the most important boat makers in the south of England.

This photograph shows the whole sweep of the Town Quay up to the Upper Wharf. It was a 'bone of contention' in the past between the Bishop of Winchester and the people of Fareham due to lack of repairs.

A postcard produced just pre-1930 when the trams were still running. Trade was so important that goods had to be overloaded often across two or three boats. Horse-drawn carts await the delivery of coal for Messers Wood and, in the background, Belvoir House still stands. The house was to come down in the 1930s.

Trading at the Lower Quay but now lorries are moving goods inland and there are more pleasure craft to be seen.

Photographed after 1976 when the tall Civic Centre had been built, Belvoir Close stands in the area of the original Belvoir House and pleasure craft now abound.

The old Gosport Road seen in 1968 after two more attempts to improve the curve of the road approaching the viaduct for Portland Street. The house directly facing us is Elmhurst.

Messers See's. Specialisation and innovation was the motto of this boat building firm. They developed speedboats and built the boat in which the Hon. Mrs Victor Bruce broke the cross-Channel record. See's also put compasses into speedboats.

The Local Quay was almost a village in its own right with a large group of Tudor cottages and four pubs. Flooding was likely at high tide. The large house is Prospect house owned by one of the many ship-building families.

THE QUAY. FAREHAM

SIDNEY
PHOTO

Looking here from the recreation ground towards the many ships on the Upper Wharf we note that swimming was always a part of the local scene.

The Lower Wharf fell badly into disrepair and was bought by 'Tug' Wilson (conditional on repair) for conversion to a marina. When repairing commenced it was found that there was a second wooden wharf lying six feet under the surface and pile driving was a nightmare. Work took place in 1966.

Opposite above: This was a sad day for Fareham. Mr Hilton Heaseman finally had to close the flour mill. Its original site was in Mill Lane but this was taken down and the bricks were used on the new mill from where flour could be sent by boat. Lorries, however, were rapidly taking over delivery.

Opposite below: The final day at the flour mill in 1960 with Mr Heaseman (centre) and his loyal longserving staff. Behind all these buildings stand three more old buildings and some ground originally used by the Royal Navy. The clearance of much of the land here revealed extensive burial grounds.

Directly on the right of this picture was where the sick and wounded were landed. The long building, once hospital wards, was destined to become a rope walk. The area was pre-Haslar and residents often found that even if they had not got a skeleton in the cupboard, they had one in the garden!

Moving now to the Upper Wharf, Messrs Hampers had a fine yacht building firm with a further section in Mill Lane. Agreement with the company that owned the cranes meant that if the Mill Lane boats needed launching the cranes must do it, so the boats were launched sideways.

The creek was gradually silting up but trading continued. Gravel boats came up to the Upper Wharf and gravel sorting went on at all hours until 1966.

In 1966 gravel sorting was abandoned after many protests about noise, and coal once again took its place. In the picture the woods and fields of Cams Hall estate can be seen.

At the Upper Wharf more changes were taking place and in 1983 we see many more pleasure craft lying by the recreation ground. Now there is a small marina here.

Apart from the Lower Wharf, flooding of the Gosport Road could also happen at high water. Here are the 'defences' after yet another road alteration in 1983.

This old postcard shows the extent of the recreation ground. It was left in perpetuity to the people of Fareham by Squire Deane of Fairfield and later Fareham House.

Driven out from their printer's shop at the bottom of Quay Street in 1983 were Harrison's the printers. Here are Ken and Iris Harrison just prior to the closure.

Looking back here to Quay Street and the Wharf is the area known (with many variations) as 'Hitch-a-Bow' corner. It was an area that was not appreciated by successive vicars being condemned as sordid and immoral. It was a smugglers' dream area even though the 'Customs' were just across the road.

Further upstream is another quay with the varying names of Bathing House, Bath House or Gas House Quay. It took its original name from the fact that there were public baths (with hot and cold water) and the latter name following the arrival of the gasometer. It is obvious that we are now reaching the end of the main shipping lane although since 1981 there have been several squabbles over the use of the quay.

One of several old German submarines which were moored in Fareham Lake after the First World War before being broken up.

Bridgefoot, Fareham   PN1452

Bridgefoot marks the end of important navigation on the river. Cams Quay in the foreground and the water have now disappeared under roadworks which started to transform this area in 1967.

Two

Changes at Bridgefoot and the Millpond

A plaque on the viaduct records the presence in the past here of the tidal mills – finally lost to Fareham in the early 1900s. It was an area busy with trade by land and water and the old A27 was a rough track.

This more recent view from the A27 was taken in the 1950s. By then the Mill Pond was silting up and getting marshy, but it could still flood at high tide when the flood waters reached Wallington. The road did not change for many years and the Mill Pond was always a centre for aggrieved Farehamites who though nothing of putting into the pond things, or even people, which they didn't want, or with whom they disagreed.

Opposite above: The River Wallington retained its old course up to 1967 and if tides were high, regularly flooded the lower gardens in High Street and the Shore road and cottages in Wallington. This sometimes still occurs now! These high waters were a boon to smugglers.

Opposite below: The Mill Pond and upper reaches around it at low tide.

This is a view of the same area at the start of the changes in the Creek and Mill Pond. Infilling has begun and Cams Quay has disappeared.

A last view of a full Mill Pond. The house was known as St Edith's Church of England Home for Girls and is now the Roundabout Hotel.

The start of changing the course of the River Wallington. Cars coming down East Street frequently failed to take the 'dog leg' at the bottom and in 1967 this happened to a large crane and some delighted young Farehamites watched as it sank slowly into the marsh!

Draining and dredging the Mill Pond. The road is the A27.

The impact of change on Quay Street. In one morning in May 1968 several buildings were demolished together to start the construction of Eastern Way.

Looking back at Quay Street with 'Tug' Wilson's and the Register Office in the background.

Eastern Way progresses, cutting through back gardens in East Street. In the background the Chequers pub can be seen.

Finally, Eastern Way reaches the creek and the A27.

The River Wallington has changed its course at the start of the huge 'Delmé' roundabout.

The roads are in use and this view together with the previous one (taken from the railway line in the twenty minute gap between trains!) gives some idea of the rising land on which Fareham is built. This part of Fareham has changed dramatically.

Three

Roads to the Town

A widened Gosport Road near the Bird in Hand, photographed in 1993.

The peace of Fareham and its surroundings was shattered in 1950 when, after a series of small explosions, two enormous explosions occurred and a mushroom-like cloud rose to 6,000 feet into the sky as barges at Bedenham (an ammunition depot between Fareham and Gosport) blew up. The blast from the explosion was funnelled up the creek and shattered many windows in West Street, broke down doors and brought down ceilings. It was at this time that Cams Hall lost its ceilings.

Quay Street, showing its old grain storages, before 1966. Georgian houses – Millards – and a small shop called 'Clacks' which was once Fareham's first telephone exchange can also be seen.

This is another clear view of Quay Street. The white wall indicates the presence of more cottages. When it was taken down an old hidden staircase was found.

Above: A closer view of Millards. A passage was also found in the building leading straight to the Upper Wharf (more smuggling?).

Left: An early view of the old Council Offices partly hidden behind a large tree in Quay Street.

The old Register Office in Quay Street – a delightful Georgian house – had to give way to traffic changes.

In the place of the old Register Office, the houses of Quay Street gave way to an unofficial parking lot. The new Police Station (1983) replaced Clark's Yard in the following picture.

Left: This view of Clark's Yard (1962), built of the famous 'Fareham Red' bricks, provides an excellent example of a droke (passage) which led to a court of approximately forty cottages. All were pulled down to make room for the police station.

Below: Turning to old Portland Street, which had now almost disappeared, we see the original tramlines which once provided the means of transport to and from Gosport.

The busy and prosperous Portland Street had a grain merchant, a pub (the Toby Jug) and a wholesale grocer selling wines and spirits.

This is the Presbytery of the church of The Sacred Heart which cuts between Portland Street and Hartlands Road.

Left: Eastern Way was opened in 1981 and about the only way to cross it is by a high footbridge, a very difficult walk for older residents. Lower Portland Street has now been demolished.

Below: Gradually, Portland Street is disappearing – the bus station wall has gone and so has the Toby Jug though the Portland still remains. Car parks are now springing up everywhere.

Right: A general view of Portland Street, looking up the street and photographed in 1994, shows the loss of homes and shops. Portland Street is destined to disappear in future developments.

Below: In Hartlands Road we saw early the signs of change when the road cottages came down in 1962. They were temporarily replaced by a shop owned by a building firm but that also came down for the building of Eastern Way.

Above: A much truncated Hartlands Road leading to the town and the new bus station.

Left: The Roman Catholic Sacred Heart church which was just over 100 years old in 1962. Built of flints, it was the result of sustained effort by local Roman Catholics who had to worship over a shop in West Street. Due to the efforts of Mr Sandy, the site was purchased. Now it stands isolated by the traffic.

Opposite above: Looking down Hartlands Road – showing the new gardens of Westbury Manor Museum and the new bus station. In 1994, 'confusion' was a mild word to describe the effect of suddenly allowing traffic to flow both ways! Naturally this happened on a Monday – market day!

Opposite below: The top of Hartlands Road in 1992. Opposite is the old post office. The walls of Westbury Manor have now been torn down as has the shop and the old solicitor's office.

Turning now to East Street, this is an old photo by George Privett showing flooding in the area from Bath Lane.

The same area is now paved. Fine Georgian houses on the approach to the Red Lion, and nearby is Fareham House.

Fareham House has become the home of Wykeham House – the school – and so has changed its name. The same thing has happened at 69, High Street. I dread to think of the problems for future historians! The junction of East Street and Bath Lane, originally Fairfield House land, led to the public baths on the quay.

The Cedar Garage twenty years ago. It has now disappeared and blocks of flats are in its place. Earlier it had been a cafe and earlier still, a part of the Fairfield estate.

Back to the old Mill Pond. Here, in 1967, Cams Hall and the Delmé Arms, once on the A27, are cut off from the new road, now a dual carriageway.

The new A27 with Fareham Girls' Grammar School in the background.

Right: Old Cams Hill.

Below: The end of Cams Hall lodges when fifteen acres of the estate were lost to the new A27.

The old Horse and Groom which became the Delmé Arms.

Old Cams Hill. The Fareham Girls' Grammar School in the background celebrates the fortieth anniversary of its opening, this year (1996).

Four

The Way to Price's School

Starting at the Royal Oak at the junction of Trinity Street and West Street, we begin a gentle climb up to Park Lane.

The new Magistrates' Court, opened in 1994 and is not a popular piece of architecture. It was called many names, when being built, very few of them complimentary!

The old Russell Way Court was demolished for newer buildings in 1994. The other 'court' had gone.

Mercifully, we still have The Sun – no longer a pub – but many, including the masters at Price's School, have memories of this 'watering hole'.

The old cottage at the corner of Colenso Road and Park Lane. Once part of the Uplands estate, it now stands on the last piece of open land which is kept for recreation.

Northwood House, once the home of Captain Miller, until he took over Uplands. Now surrounded by pleasant residential accommodations. Captain Miller owned most of the land in the area and tried to keep it open for Price's School.

Price's School, photographed from the air in 1971. The school extensions have been built, but one can see the encroaching estates in the area.

Prices School & Headmaster's House in West Street.
1721.

A sketch, which shows the original Price's Charity school and the Master's house. William Price left his money to found a charity school for thirty boys and thirty girls. He did this in a fit of pique when his sisters turned from the Anglican religion.

The old building became a ruin and a new one, with a school master's house, was built in 1845. It is interesting to note that the girls had now 'disappeared', the excuse being that no-one could be found to teach sewing and at a time when even boys were taught to knit! The school was growing and a new one, in Park Lane, was built in 1910. Next door to the empty school is the parish hall.

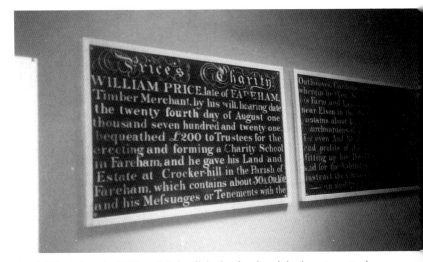

Price's School always had William Price's will displayed on boards by the entrance to the building. Fortunately these boards were saved when, in 1989, destruction of the buildings began. Earlier it had become a Sixth form college and back came the girls again but, finally the buildings and the school were lost.

The original old building – recorded here in 1989 – standing fair and square. Note the bell tower.

The college (which it had now become) grew enormously, as shown here, and in the next photograph.

The newest building stood on the site of the old laboratories. Many tales can be told of these, by old Priceans.

Destruction in 1989.

The end – August 1989. Some of the rubble ended up underneath Dean Farm Shop barn which was being built at the time.

Desolation.

The opening of the building site in 1994.

Further development. After a local 'fight' the name William Price Gardens was achieved for the new road.

Price's Lodge – the whole area.

A Leisure Centre was built almost opposite the school site. Ironically, one of the arguments put forward for the destruction of Price's School was that 'it was too far out for pupils to reach!'

Uplands, the home of Samuel Jellicoe, the Beardmores and finally, Captain Miller. It is now an old people's home.

The beautiful front of Uplands. There have been several unsuccessful attempts to get it pulled down. Wild orchids grow at the bottom of the garden.

Five

Fareham Girl's Grammar School

A grammar school for girls at last! Sadly its status was wrenched from it by educational changes. This is an aerial photo – 1963 – when the first extensions were in position. The large windows always leaked and the heat never reached the extensions! Note the absence of settlement in Down End and beyond.

Birdwood Grove and Rooksway were not made up for years. This is the famous puddle outside the caretaker's house.

The first members of staff in 1956: Miss M.E. Lowe (Headmistress), Miss M. Rush (Senior Mistress, Head of Science), Miss E. Rymer (Head of English), Miss R. Heggie (P.E.), Miss R. Hillyard (Art and Geography), Miss M. Jubb (Mathematics), Mrs D. Crozier (Domestic Science), Mrs D. Rymer (Music), Mrs Porter (Secretary).

Two forms to start with in 1956. The rubble heaps made exciting places to dig for flints and for the hoped for road from Portchester.

'Break' taken in the first week of the school.

School buses were essential as the school was so far out of town. Note the gabardines and the berets. Heaven help you if you were caught without your beret!

Our 'gentleman of the road'. The first crossing patrol man was the much loved Mr McCarthy who died suddenly in 1962.

The official opening of the school in 1957 with, from left to right: Mr Lubbock, Mr Munday, Miss Lowe, Bishop of Portsmouth, the Rt. Revd L. Scott-Fleming, Mrs Dyke.

Miss Rymer's and Miss Rush's 2nd Forms in 1956/57.

The 2nd Forms again in 1956/57. Can you find yourself or recognise anyone?

A school outing.

Two members of staff and three girls in 1956. Do you recognise any of them?

The first 'Fareham Past and Present' exhibition in 1960. The school was filled!

The enlargement of the school, with senior forms, brought a new influx of staff by 1958.

There was happy collaboration (in more ways than one!) between the school and Price's School. Several joint Gilbert and Sullivan operettas were put on and this one was HMS Pinafore.

Six

Some of Fareham's Other Schools

An old private school was Miss Kiln's school in Portland Street.

Form 2 of the local Church of England School in 1946.

Grade 7 of the Church of England School in 1946.

An aerial view of Wallisdean School with extensions. Flat roofs were all the rage!

Form 3B at Fareham County Primary School (possibly in 1951). The teacher was Mrs Hillyard.

Left: The senior part of Wykeham House School at 69 High Street in 1968. Note the magnificent doorway and the worn step. This is now known as Fareham House to add to the confusion for future historians! *Right*: The Junior part of Wykeham House School at 67, High Street. with its magnificent door and ironwork.

Fathers' Race at Wykeham House Sports Day before 1966. The sports field was on the Wickham Road and was lost when Wallington Way was built.

Spectators at Wykeham House Sports Day. Note the boaters.

Now Wykeham House School this is the famous Fareham House in East Street, home of several naval families in the past. It was taken over by the Ministry of Employment during the Second World War.

Mrs James asks 'who are these miscreants?'

Seven

The Golden Mile
– West Street

The famous coaching inn, the Red Lion, stands proudly at the junction of East, West and High Street.

Old West Street in 1962 – still unchanged. Looking west from the Red Lion, several famous family firms are still in position. Look at the second storeys, many are basically Tudor and appear to 'lean' on one another.

Looking back in the opposite direction, the wide West Street is unchanged and so are the shops. This was 1962 and changes were on the way.

Another part of West Street unchanged in 1960. Readers may recognise the White House, the old post office and the two cinemas, as well as Parker's Dairy shop.

Changes had started with the development of the precinct and the pedestrianisation of the wide part of West Street and the family-run shops began to close. Here in 1982, Burt the butcher had gone and Waters the fishmonger was closing, after three generations.

Vimpany, the jeweller, across the street, had held out until 1982. It was the last shop with shutters. Postal deliveries were once taken in here and the Tudor walls had to be shored up when the next shop was rebuilt.

A little further west – more empty shops and the 'creeping paralysis' of the precinct can be seen. There is an entry which masks one of the altered 'drokes'.

The four-storey Batchelors, a chemist for 200 hundred years, is now a building society office and Silvers, an outfitters, well known to Price's School boys, is about to close in 1996.

The junction with West Street and Quay Street in 1962. Bussey, the butcher, Hayward, the greengrocer and Hinxman, the car firm, had gone by 1995.

Hinxman's was once Coles, the coachbuilders and coachmakers to George IV. They were once fined seven shillings and sixpence for causing a traffic jam with display coaches in the road. Haywards, the little Tudor shop, was probably the oldest shop in Fareham, its deeds went back to the 1400s.

Pedestrianisation in 1981 shows the same area but with changes.

Hinxman, Hayman and others have now gone as this is 1991. West Street is partially pedestrianised. Note the Queen Victoria plaque on the big house next to The Crown.

The same area from the opposite angle in 1991. Inevitably a car park has now appeared here.

Taken twenty years earlier, it is worth having a look at this delightful Tudor shop with its original clapper boarding. There will never be another one like it.

The delightful old United Reformed church, not now used for services, still stands. It backs onto the market place – look at the flowers.

A montage of West Street In 1976. Here we still have some old and well-known shops.

The market isn't what it was. Photographed in 1981, lost already is the famous animal market now replaced by stalls of clothes, greengroceries etc. Even these will soon be lost by proposed new developments of this area.

The market on any day except Monday, but now a car park bounded by Quay Street and Portland Street. Note the enormous roundabout island into which as many as seven roads feed.

An aerial view looking south to the coast. High Street (centre) is still intact at this time. (Photo by R. Aylott)

Another photograph by Bob Aylott taken in 1981. The flat roofs show the extent of the present buildings. The Medical Centre is in the foreground.

Another use for a pedestrian precinct! Note the new shopping centre and the old bus station. This was in 1981 and 'quality' shops were beginning to disappear. (Photo by R. Aylott)

Another part of the precinct. The fire station has become Manpower. The old Fareham well was found just outside here. The Parish Hall is King Brothers, but has since become yet another building society office. (Photo by R. Aylott)

A unique photograph which cannot be taken again from the same angle. This magnificent landscape photograph was taken by Innes Marlow from the top of Holy Trinity church spire just before the spire was pulled down in 1992. West Street and Osborn Road can be seen and the Civic Centre.

The builders of Fareham fire station which was opened in 1911. Back row, left to right: F. Bath, H. Lambden, A. Limburn, W. Sansom, B. Biggs, F. Frost, G. Jeffrey. Centre row: F.G. Shepherd, J. Langford, E. Mason, H. Harvey, J. Glover, C. Knight, T. Ayres, F. Smith, W. Hoare, J. Lewis. Front row: W. Langford, F. Wells, W. Grant, H. Longman, W.H. Glover, A. Misslebrook, F. Biggs, H. Fielder.

The old bus station looking towards Portland Street, 1981. To build this, three cottages, one a lending library, and one the home of Thackeray's great aunt, were pulled down. The roof slates were reused on the station.

The bus station is now another car park. The Sacred Heart church is in the background.

The white building was originally Jeffery's furniture shop, pulled down in 1993. Next to it is Westbury Manor here starting a new life as a museum.

Old Westbury Manor estate in 1962 with the house and ornate walls. The door marks the solicitor's office which for years was the legal centre for Stewards of Cams Manor. Deeds going back to 1660 were found.

Recorded in 1992, the old office has gone and so has much of the wall.

The old wall and solicitor's office came down in 1993, ready for the new gardens of Westbury Manor Museum.

The museum is now, in 1993 nearly complete on the outside. Jeffery's has been pulled down.

A view of the museum gardens taken in 1994. In the background is the old post office – now a building society office.

An interesting remnant of old Fareham was Westbury farm in Westbury Alley. Unfortunately, vandals destroyed it in 1996.

Left: Malthouse Lane with its 'court' of cottages was demolished in 1962. Mr Whiting, the sweep, lived up here. Part of this scene can still be located by the house in the background which is passed on entering Osborn Road South car park. *Right:* The last of our cinemas, the Embassy, came down in 1983. Thanks to fore-warning by the cinema manager and help from Mr Croad, valuable material and machinery were recovered which is now in the museum, from where this picture was taken.

Older West Street just after the Second World War, showing the two cinemas, the Embassy and the Savoy. The latter is in the group of white buildings in the centre. The house on the left was a dentist's, appropriately, Mr Butcher!

The end of the Embassy cinema in 1983.

A quality grocers was Messrs Stone. This picture, taken in 1948, shows five well-known girls who served in the shop: Muriel Wells, Marjorie Bone, Connie Warner, Winnie Early and Joan Bell. Connie may be known to many as Mrs Etherington, of Dean Farm and the farm shop.

These shops and building society offices were where the old shop by Malt House Lane stood. Many buildings were still there in 1981, but changed hands very rapidly.

This and the next photograph show contrasting features. This is Admiral's Row in 1982. The second stories give some clue to the age of the buildings once largely occupied by naval families.

Above: The opposite side shows modernity setting in, though it is sometimes possible to see the old houses behind. Traffic rules have altered. Coming from the railway station you must now go up Trinity Street, along Osborn Road and down Osborn Road South to get back into West Street. Buses can take a short cut!

Left: The end of Holy Trinity church spire in 1992. The spire used to be a landmark for boats coming up the creek. Oddly, the spire was not part of the original building.

Above: Approaching the railway station road. Bridge widening resulted in the 'new' West End Hotel being demolished, as has happened to its predecessor. Lost with it were Cremer Cottages (not shown). These were set up by Sir William Cremer, Nobel Prize winner. He also set up the International Court at the Hague.

Right: Holy Trinity church without its spire.

The old Railway Hotel which came down in the 1950s. It was the scene of much fun and games at Christmas with the so-called 'Fareham Hunt' and such 'tribal rites' as scattering small coins and sweets out of the windows for the children.

In its place came the Crown Bingo Club, as well as many alternatives before it became the Bingo hall. This scene is from 1981.

The station entrance in 1901 - a much widened street and a roundabout. Part of the new fire station can be seen on the right.

The sign reads BEWARE ONCOMING BUSES IN THE MIDDLE OF THE ROAD. Double decker buses could not pass except in the middle – height restriction! The cottages had been pulled down to enable the road to be widened and a new bridge built in 1968.

Fareham Railway Station in Coronation Year, 1953, with a steam train taking on water.

G.A. Day's at the corner of Quay Street being restored after a fire.

The old fire station is now a cafe. Both the above photographs were taken in 1996.

Eight

Some Social Events

Trinity Street VE Day party held behind the old Church House.

The VE Day street party at Paxton Road.

Christmas Day at the Railway Hotel for the so-called 'Fareham hunt' – a motley lot who never caught anything!

This is believed to be a Victory party held at Holy Trinity Church House.

The 'Fanciers' draw at the Royal Oak. Mrs Lawrence holds the bouquet.

Knowle patients' sports day on the cricket field before the Second World War. The three children are, left to right: Stan Ford, Joan Watts and Ralph Ford.

Rabbits! The date and the people are not known, can you help?

Mr Shawyer with his winning racing pigeon.

The staff of Phillips, the dress shop, photographed on a day out in the early 1950s.

Conversation piece at the Horticultural Show in 1991. Centre is the late lamented 'Harry' Swatton.

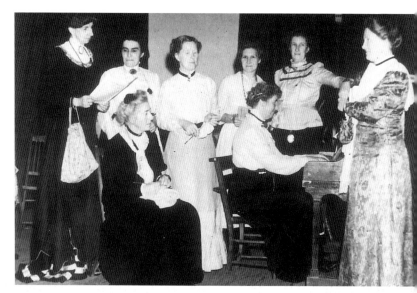

Another conversation piece? The date of this photograph is not known but left to right are: Miss Hackney, Mrs Albrow, Mrs Cussons, Mrs Mann, Mrs Winnett (piano), Mrs Isaacs, Mrs Paterson, Miss Bromhead.

Nine

High Street – Unchanging

The bottom of the High Street in 1962. Little changed really but Edney's have moved and Ayres (photographers) have closed.

Further up the High Street in 1964. The County Club with its double bays is now a restaurant. Wykeham House School (double roofed), 69, High Street was a school until 1986. The battered stables were restored. Note the fine Kintyre House, once the home of Admiral Donaldson.

The bottom of the High Street in 1982. Note the original balustrade over what used to be a tobacconist's. The larger shop was once known as the 'Little Dustpan'.

No. 12 High Street with its coach entrance in 1966.

Nos 15 to 17 in 1964. Note the 'irregularities' of style.

Nos 17 to 19 High Street in 1967. The curved top wall marks the site of the old Coach and Horses.

Nearing the top of the street looking north in 1982. Note the Elizabethan cottages and the Golden Lion at the top.

The top of the street, eastern side, in 1902. Both shops have changed hands and Mr Collins, the butcher, no longer keeps an eye on his shop from the Golden Lion!

Looking down what is actually 'Vicar's Hill'. The houses at the bottom were pulled down and rebuilt.

Lower High Street, north, and the old Vicarage, hence 'Vicar's Hill'. Like all houses on that side of the road, it had a passage down to the creek for the smugglers' runs at high water.

Nos 23 to 25 in 1964. Elizabethan cottages have seen several changes in use as shops in recent years.

Proof of the name 'Vicar's Hill'.

The old post office at the junction of Osborn Road and Wickham Road in the early years of this century. It was built on what was a pond on the 'Hog Plat', spare land used for archery practice.

Ten

The Rise of the Phoenix – Cams Hall

Lying just off the A27 stands Cams Hall. Here, seen in 1961, it was derelict and suffering from neglect. The Bedenham explosion had brought the ceilings down and the lead had been stolen from the roof.

G & F Beagles at Cams Hall, Jan 29th 1909.

Here it is at the height of prosperity. It had the most beautiful landscaped gardens and was a centre for social life. The owners owned vast areas of land extending from Portchester to well beyond Wickham, being Lords of several manors.

Part of the huge kitchen garden.

The Delmé family's male heirs had died out and in a fit of pique the last one sold up. It was bought by Montague Foster who rented it out. During the Second World War it was taken over by Portsmouth Naval authorities. It was earlier sold to Jonathan May who intended to build up a housing estate but was prevented from doing this by the Bedenham explosion.

The land was farmed by the Hill family and the old farm courtyard buildings fell derelict.

In the 1950s a caravan park was started.

Gradually, the weather did its worst to all the buildings.

The wonderful coach shelter built by H.P. Delmé fell into disrepair after the Hills left.

More devastation.

Yet more damage caused by the hurricane in 1987.

The Orangery was vandalised and eventually disappeared.

The wonderful stables and their arches held firm. These came from Titchfield.

There were many plans to develop the estate but these were thwarted by lack of money and planning permission until Mr Church stepped in and up went the scaffolding.

Masses of scaffolding at the front and sides.

Left: Scaffolding at the back. Unfortunately, Mr Church was killed when his plane crashed but the work was taken over by Strand Harbour Securities.

Below: We watched breathlessly as Messrs Waring applied their renovating skills and the following photographs show the progress made.

Opposite above: The repaired coach shed.

Opposite below: The repaired farmhouse and tidy farm yard.

The coachman's house and stables.

The repaired coachman's house.

The stone building to the right of the coachman's house might have once been a chapel.

The repaired courtyard.

The walled garden building being tidied up. Note the large stone sink.

Cams Hall, restored and standing on its 'lofty eminence'. The farm lands are now a golf course.

The view from Cams Hall, looking back to the viaduct, the creek and the Delme Arms.

Finally, we have come full circle. A view from the great meadow overlooking Fareham Quay in 1981. You may recognise the Quays, though the boats are now pleasure craft instead of trading ships.

Acknowledgements

The greater number of photographs come from my very large collection of cards, slides and personal photographs, gathered over many years.

I wish to acknowledge contributions from the following: Robert Aylott, photographer, Mr C. Baxandall, Mrs Bell, Mrs R. Billett, especially for her photographs of Price's School and Fareham Girls' Grammar School, Mr Coker, Mr G. Croad, Mrs A. Edds, Fareham Borough Council, Mr R. Ford, Mr R. Grant, Mrs Hartley, Mrs Harper, Mr Hawkins, Mr F. Hoare, Mrs Jones, Mrs Lawrence, Mrs Madden, Mr Innes Marlow, Mr Newman, Mrs O. Palmer and the staff of Westbury Manor Museum, Mr A. Penford and the staff of Hampshire County Museum Service at Chilcomb, especially Mr T. Evans and Mr B. Holmes. Mr G. Rogers, Mr Sanders, Mr K. Shawyer, Mrs Sims, Mr S. Waring of Strand Harbour Securities for allowing us to wander all over the Cams estate, Mrs E. Wright. Photographers no longer with us include, Messrs Brown, Crouch, G. and M. Privett, Garrad, J.C. Draper and H. Sturgess.

Finally, for the constant help of my husband. After my accident resulting in a spell in hospital, I could never have finished this book without the help of transport and the friendship of 'Jessica'. Without her, we should not been able to complete this book in time.

Further Reading

G. Privett, *The Story of Fareham*
R. Aylott (and A. James), *Fareham Two Views*
R.A. Stone, *The Meon Valley Railway*
J. Emery, *Fareham in Old Picture Postcards*
A. James, *Fareham between the Wars*
P. Moore, *Bygone Fareham*
A. James, *Our Beloved Fareham*
L. Burton and B. Musselwhite, *An Illustrated History of Fareham*